OXFORD BOOKWORMS LIBRARY

Factfiles

Muha

ANDREA SARTO

Stage 2 (700 headwords)

Series Editor: Rachel Bladon

Founder Factfiles Editor: Christine Lindop

OXFORD
UNIVERSITY PRESS

Great Clarendon Street, Oxford, OX2 6DP, United Kingdom

Oxford University Press is a department of the University of Oxford. It furthers the University's objective of excellence in research, scholarship, and education by publishing worldwide. Oxford is a registered trade mark of Oxford University Press in the UK and in certain other countries

First published 2018

10 9 8 7 6 5 4 3 2 1

ISBN: 978 0 19 462434 3 Book

A complete recording of this Bookworms edition of *Muhammad Ali* is available.

Printed in China

Word count (main text): 7,419

For more information on the Oxford Bookworms Library, visit www.oup.com/elt/gradedreaders

ACKNOWLEDGEMENTS

Cover Image: Alamy Stock Photo (Muhammad Ali/Trinity Mirror/Mirrorpix).

The publisher would like to thank the following for the permission to reproduce photographs: Alamy Stock Photo pp.32 (Ali in Zaire/Everett Collection Inc), 44 (Muhammad Ali Center/Thomas Kelley); Getty Images pp.0 (Muhammad Ali/Michael Cooper), 6 (young Muhammad Ali/Bettmann), 9 (Sugar Ray Robinson/George Karger), 10 (1960 Summer Olympics/Jerry Cooke), 12 (boxers at 1960 Olympics/Jerry Cooke), 14 (Ali boxing/Hy Peskin), 15 (Sonny Liston/The Stanley Weston Archive), 16 (Muhammad Ali and Malcolm X/Bob Gomel), 17 (Muhammad Ali vs Sonny Liston/ Neil Leifer), 18 (Muhammad Ali vs Sonny Liston/Neil Leifer), 23 (Ali talks to press/A. Y. Owen), 24 (Martin Luther King/New York Daily News Archive), 28 (Ali dodging punch/Bettmann), 29 (Ali press conference/Popperfoto), 31 (George Foreman press conference/Bettmann), 34 (Ali vs George Foreman/Neil Leifer), 35 (Ali and President Ford/Bettmann), 36 (Ali, Frazier and King/Neil Leifer), 39 (Ali vs Frazier/Bettmann), 42 (Ali and Royce Smart/MARIA BASTONE), 43 (Ali film poster/ John D. Kisch/Separate Cinema Archive), 45 (Ali and wife/Chris Weeks), 60 (Ali vs Cleveland Williams/Neil Leifer), 64 (Serena Williams/Pool); Press Association Images pp.5 (policeman and Ali/Chas. Kays/The Courier-Journal-USA TODAY Sports), 20 (Ali interview/Robert Steinau/The Courier-Journal-USA TODAY Sports); Rex Shutterstock pp.3 (tributes to Ali/ddp USA), 4 (young Muhammad Ali/REX/Shutterstock), 19 (civil rights march/Underwood Archives), 26 (Joe Frazier/ Associated Newspapers), 27 (boxing match poster/Startraks Photo), 36 (Ali vs Frazier poster/ REX/Shutterstock), 41 (Ali on aeroplane/Associated Newspapers), 46 (signed boxing glove/REX/ Shutterstock), 47 (Muhammad Ali funeral/Jonathan Palmer/ZUMA Wire), 49 (Ali in London/ Gibson/Associated Newspapers), 52 (Ali vs Spinks/Colorsport).

Content Editor: Nicole Irving

The author would like to dedicate this book to his friend, Dr Charles Nduka.

CONTENTS

1 "The Greatest"

It is 1996, in Atlanta, Georgia, USA. A man walks slowly into the Olympic stadium. Everyone waits. Who is it? The people in the crowd shout when they see the man's face on the large TVs around the stadium. It is a big surprise.

The man's hands and arms are shaking because he is sick, but he holds up a torch to the crowd, and it burns brightly. It is the Olympic torch, gold against the night sky.

More than three billion people around the world are watching this man, on TV and in the stadium, and nearly all of them know his name. He is one of the most famous men in the world. He is Muhammad Ali – "The Greatest."

* * *

That day in Atlanta, Ali did not look strong. He was fifty-four years old, and he was sick with Parkinson's disease. But he was still famous as a boxer who won many important fights. He was famous as a man who won other hard, important fights, too – for black people's rights and for peace. So how did Ali's great life journey begin? And how did he become "The Greatest," and a hero to people around the world?

2 Early years

On January 17, 1942, fifty-four years before that night at the Atlanta Olympics, Muhammad Ali was born in Louisville, Kentucky, USA. But "Muhammad Ali" was not his name then – his mother and father's last name was Clay, and they gave him the first name Cassius.

Cassius Clay's father was a loud, fast talker, and his mother was kind and warm. He had one younger brother called Rudolph, and the Clay family lived in a small house on Grand Avenue in the center of the city of Louisville. The brothers often played in the street, and sometimes, Cassius asked Rudolph to throw stones at him. Cassius loved trying to move away from the stones quickly – and Rudolph could never hit him because he was so fast.

At that time, life in Louisville was hard for black people. In the south of the USA in the 1940s and 1950s, black people did not have equal rights with white people. Black people had to sit at the back of buses, and restaurants did not sell them food. There were different schools for black children and white children, too, and black people usually had to do the hardest jobs for not much money.

One day, Cassius was at a bus stop with his mother. It was very hot and he wanted to get a cup of water from a restaurant near the bus stop. But the people in the restaurant did not give him any water because he was black. Cassius began crying and said that he was thirsty,

The Clay family home on Grand Avenue, Louisville

but nobody listened, and his mother had to take him away.

Cassius always remembered this, and when he was older, he wanted to make life better for black people – "my people,"[1] he called them. Sometimes, when he was still a young boy, he woke up in the middle of the night. He went outside and looked up at the stars, and he thought about what he wanted to do in his life. He was ready to do "great things,"[2] he said, and he wanted to try and make changes in the world.

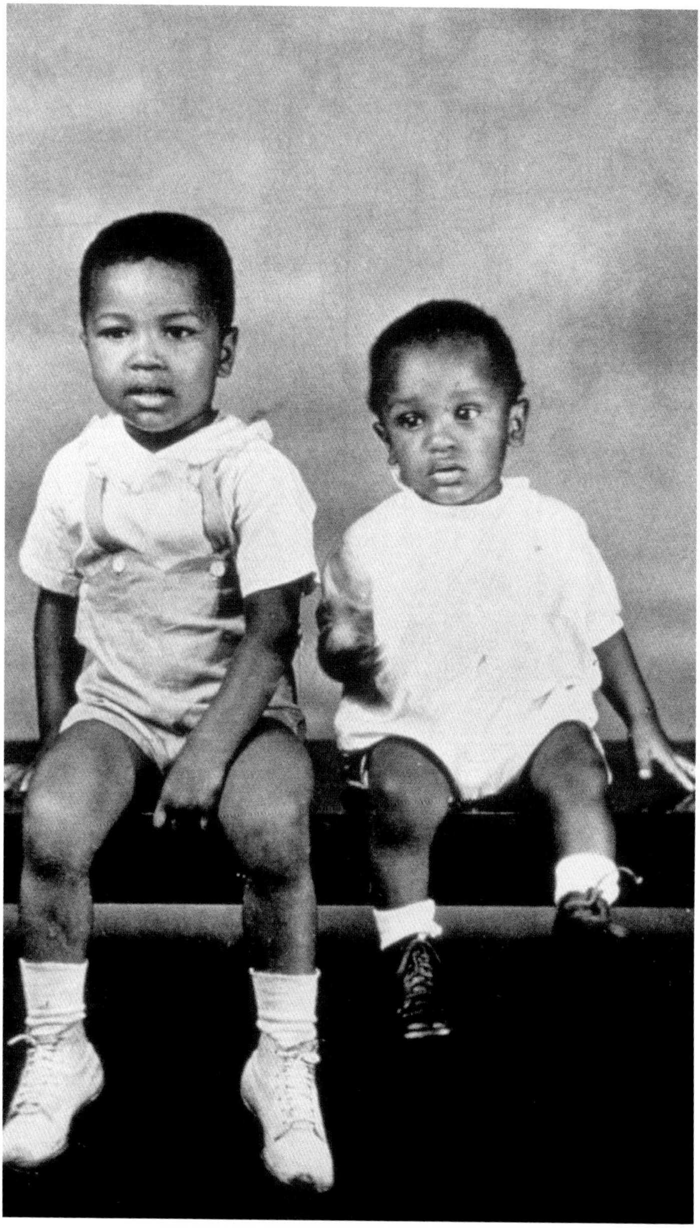

Young Cassius Clay (left) with his brother Rudolph

* * *

An important thing happened one afternoon in October 1954, when Cassius was twelve years old. He went into Louisville on his new red-and-white bicycle, and left it outside a theater. But a thief took it, so when Cassius came back later, the bicycle was not there. Cassius cried and was angry, but then someone said to him, "Go and see Joe Martin, the police officer. He's working in the gym down the street."

Joe Martin was teaching boxing to young boys in the gym. Cassius wanted to find the bicycle thief and fight him – and he told Joe this. But Joe said to Cassius that he must first learn to fight. Joe Martin did not know at that time how important his words were: Cassius's life as a boxer began after the meeting with Joe that day.

Joe Martin and
Cassius Clay, 1959

At first, Joe thought that Cassius was nothing special – he had thin legs and arms, and did not look very strong. But soon, Joe could see how hard Cassius worked in the gym. He was there six days a week.

Joe could also see how Cassius moved fast or "danced" around the boxing ring. In boxing, you need to punch the other fighter and then move away quickly, so "dancing" like this is a good thing.

Six weeks after he started to box, young Cassius Clay won his first fight against another boy from Louisville. After the fight, he said to everyone that he was "The Greatest" and that one day, he would become the World Champion!

At school, Cassius was not a strong student – he usually did not do well in class. But his boxing got better and better, and more people in Louisville began to hear about him. Once, his picture was in the newspaper after a fight.

Cassius was very proud. He got lots of newspapers and cut out the pictures from them to keep.

Not everyone was happy for Cassius. There was a young man in Louisville called Corky Baker, who did not like it when other people did well. Corky was very strong, and everyone was afraid of him. Sometimes he hit Cassius's friends in the street. Cassius was very angry about this. He wanted to help his friends, so he decided to fight Corky – not in the street or at school, but in the boxing ring. Corky agreed.

At the start of the fight, Cassius's legs were shaking, but after the first round, he was too fast for Corky. He punched Corky hard and, in the end, Corky ran out of the ring and the gym. Corky did not hit Cassius's friends again after this. "We're free!" they shouted happily.

Cassius fought 108 fights and won ten big competitions before his eighteenth birthday. This is a lot in just a few years. Some of the competitions were in big American cities like Chicago. Other boxers who won these competitions soon became very rich and famous. Was this the way forward for Cassius Clay, too?

Cassius Clay, age 12

3 Going for gold

In 1960, Cassius Clay won the chance to box for the USA at the Olympics. For an eighteen-year-old from Louisville, this was wonderful. But Cassius was afraid of flying – and the 1960 Olympics were in Rome, Italy.

At first, Cassius did not want to go. But Joe Martin, his trainer, did not want Cassius to lose the chance to be a great fighter. They went for a long walk together around Louisville and talked a lot. In the end, Cassius agreed – he would go to Rome, he told Joe.

Nine Olympic boxers from the USA met in New York City before they flew to Rome. Cassius loved being in New York. The city was so big and busy, with so many people – and he wanted to talk to everyone. In the evening, he went with some of the other boxers to the restaurant of a famous black boxer called Sugar Ray Robinson. Sugar Ray was Cassius's hero, and Cassius wanted to see him and get his autograph. He wanted to see Sugar Ray's car, too, which was pink and very expensive! Cassius wanted to buy a big, expensive car, but at that time, he still did not have a lot of money.

When Sugar Ray arrived at the restaurant, Cassius went to speak to him. But Sugar Ray just said, "Later, boy; I'm busy right now."[3] Cassius was unhappy about this. When he was a great boxer, he decided, he would talk to everyone and always give people his autograph!

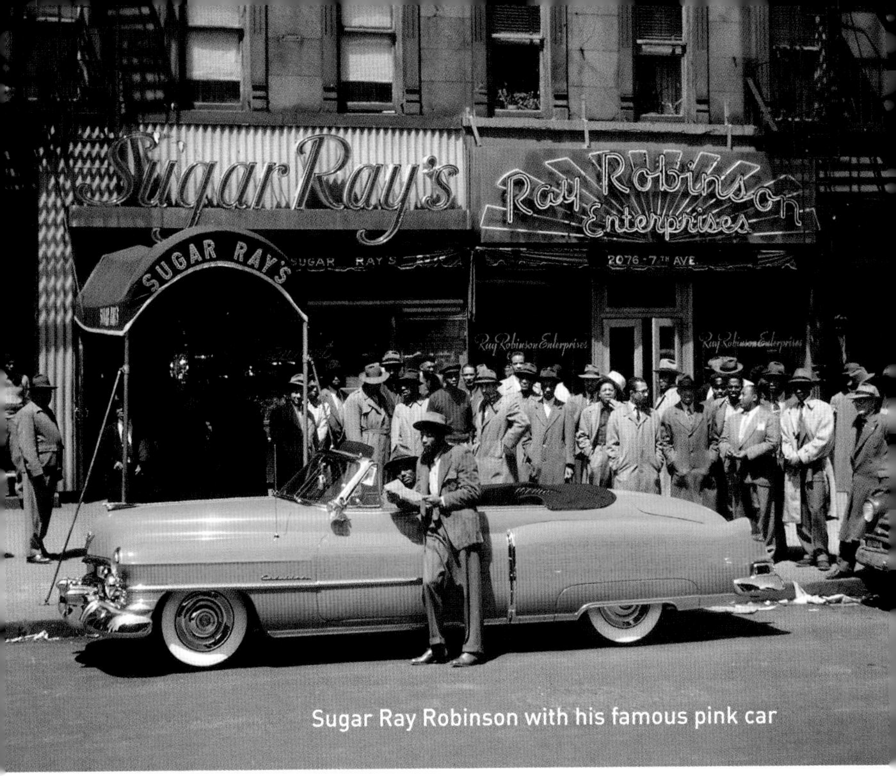

Sugar Ray Robinson with his famous pink car

After dinner that night, Cassius saw a black man in the street outside the restaurant. He was holding a piece of paper which said, "BUY BLACK." He wanted people to buy things from black people's stores, not white people's stores. This surprised Cassius. In Louisville, black people did not say things like this; they could not because they were too afraid.

On the plane to Rome, Cassius and the other boxers spoke about medals. For all of that long journey, Cassius did not stop talking about how he wanted a gold medal. His friends knew that he was talking so much because he was afraid of flying!

In the Olympic Village in Rome, Cassius soon became very popular. He said hello to everybody, asked their names, and shook their hands. He told them about himself and said that he wanted to win a gold medal in boxing. Deep inside, he knew that he would get gold, and he told people this. He also trained very hard.

During the competition, he won against three other boxers because he was too fast for them. And then, to win the gold medal, he had to fight the European Champion – a boxer from Poland called Zbigniew Pietrzykowski. The Polish boxer was seven years older than Cassius Clay, and he had a dangerous left punch.

There were three rounds in the fight, and each round was three minutes long. In Rounds 1 and 2, Pietrzykowski

was very strong. Was the Polish boxer too good for Clay? Did he want the gold medal more? In Round 3, both boxers fought well, but in the last minute, Clay hit Pietrzykowski hard. The Polish boxer fell against the ropes that go around the ring. And then Clay hit Pietrzykowski one, two, three times with his right hand. Now Pietrzykowski's head went down, and Clay started to dance around the ring.

So, at the end of Round 3, Clay was the winner. Cassius Clay, Olympic Champion! Clay loved the shouts of the crowd, and they all loved him. The Olympics were on TV in the USA for the first time that year, and the TV cameras loved Clay, too. Suddenly, everyone was talking about this wonderful young black boxer from Louisville, Kentucky.

When Clay got back to New York, he was very proud. He walked around Times Square, the busiest place in the city, and showed people his gold medal. On the front of his coat, in big red letters, it said "USA." Clay was proud to be American. He thought that his country was the best in the world.

Pietrzykowski and Clay,
Rome Olympics, 1960

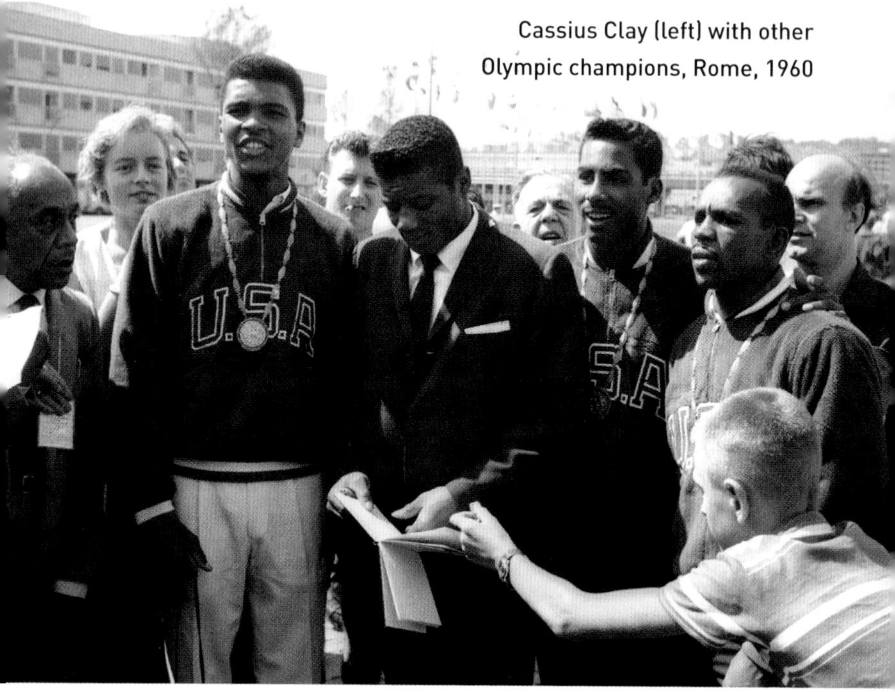

Cassius Clay (left) with other Olympic champions, Rome, 1960

In Louisville, a large crowd was waiting to see Cassius Clay when he arrived home. For the next few weeks, he took his gold medal everywhere with him. He ate with it, he slept with it. He was famous at last. His life was different and anything was possible.

But some things in Louisville did not change. When Clay and a friend went into a restaurant for white people, they still could not buy any food.

"I'm Cassius Clay. The Olympic Champion,"[4] Clay said, and showed his gold medal. But the man in the restaurant shook his head. In Louisville at that time, if you were an Olympic champion, and famous, it did not change things: for black people, life was still hard.

4 World Champion

After the 1960 Olympics, Cassius Clay began working full-time as a boxer: boxing was now his job. During the next three years, he won nineteen fights, one after another. He traveled all over the USA, and even boxed in London, England.

When he visited places, he talked about how good he was, how fast he was, and how pretty he was. Other boxers did not call themselves "pretty," but Clay had a beautiful face and he knew it. He loved playing with words and saying surprising things.

Clay also knew how to work with people from the newspapers and TV when he wanted everyone to be excited about a fight. One time, he told a photographer a big secret: to get faster, he trained underwater, he said. It was not true – he could not even swim! But because Clay said this, the photographer wanted to take pictures, so Clay agreed. Soon, there were pictures of him in all the newspapers boxing underwater.

Clay also started telling people – before a fight – the number of the winning round. The Olympic fights had only three rounds, but now Clay was fighting longer fights with a lot more rounds. Before a fight against a boxer called Archie Moore, Clay thought that he would win in Round 4, so he said, "Archie Moore will fall in four."[5] And in Round 4 of the fight, he knocked out Moore

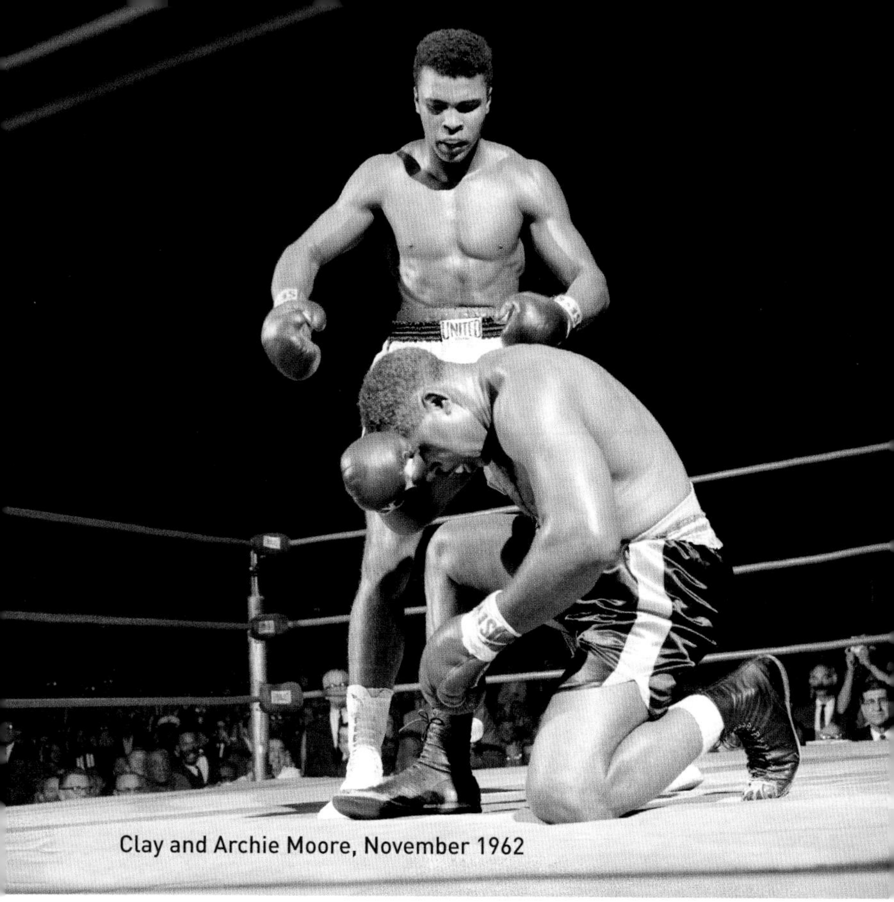
Clay and Archie Moore, November 1962

and won easily. Clay did the same thing for twelve more fights: before each of these fights, he said the number of the winning round, and he was right. A few people who did not like Clay said that he talked too much, but Clay was a new young boxer who was not afraid to be loud and proud. And when other boxers got angry outside the ring because of his talk, Clay could win more easily inside the ring.

In 1964, when Clay was twenty-two years old, he got a chance to fight the World Champion, Sonny Liston. Liston was a big, tough man with large hands, who never smiled and did not talk much. In nearly all of his fights, Liston knocked out the other boxer.

At this time, Clay had a bus to drive himself and his trainer and other people to fights. A few weeks before the Liston fight, he drove with some friends in his bus to Liston's house early in the morning. On the side of the bus were the words:

SONNY LISTON IS GREAT,
BUT HE'LL FALL IN EIGHT.[6]

Clay stopped in front of Liston's house and made a lot of noise. He shouted about how he was not afraid, but Liston told Clay and his friends to go away. People thought that Clay was crazy. Did he want Liston to get even angrier?

Most people did not think that Clay would win against Liston. One newspaper reporter had to find the way from the boxing ring to the nearest hospital before the fight. "Clay will need to go there when he loses," the people from his newspaper told him.

Sonny Liston

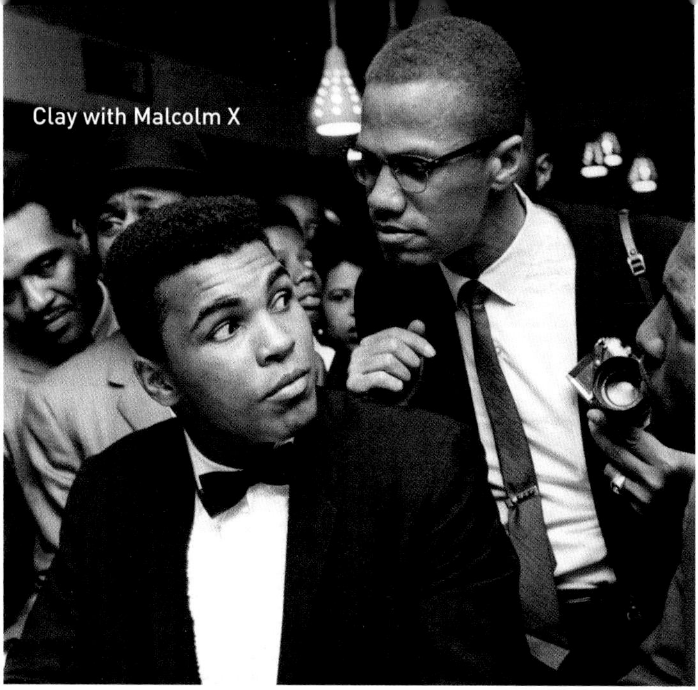

Clay with Malcolm X

One friend who *did* think Clay had a chance was Malcolm X. He was a famous speaker about black people's rights. Some people in the USA did not like him because he told black people to fight against white people who did bad things to them. But Malcom X was like an older brother to Cassius Clay. He said that Clay was young and strong, and would win for black people everywhere.

On February 25, 1964, the night of the fight, the crowd shouted for Liston. They did not like how Clay held his gloves down and danced around the ring. "When is Liston going to catch Clay with a big punch? When is he going to knock him out?" they thought. But Clay moved his head away all the time and was too fast for Liston.

In boxing, the two boxers rest for one minute between rounds. After Round 4, when Clay was resting in his corner of the ring, he said to his trainer that he could not see. He said that there was something on Liston's gloves – it was burning his eyes! Perhaps Liston's trainer put something

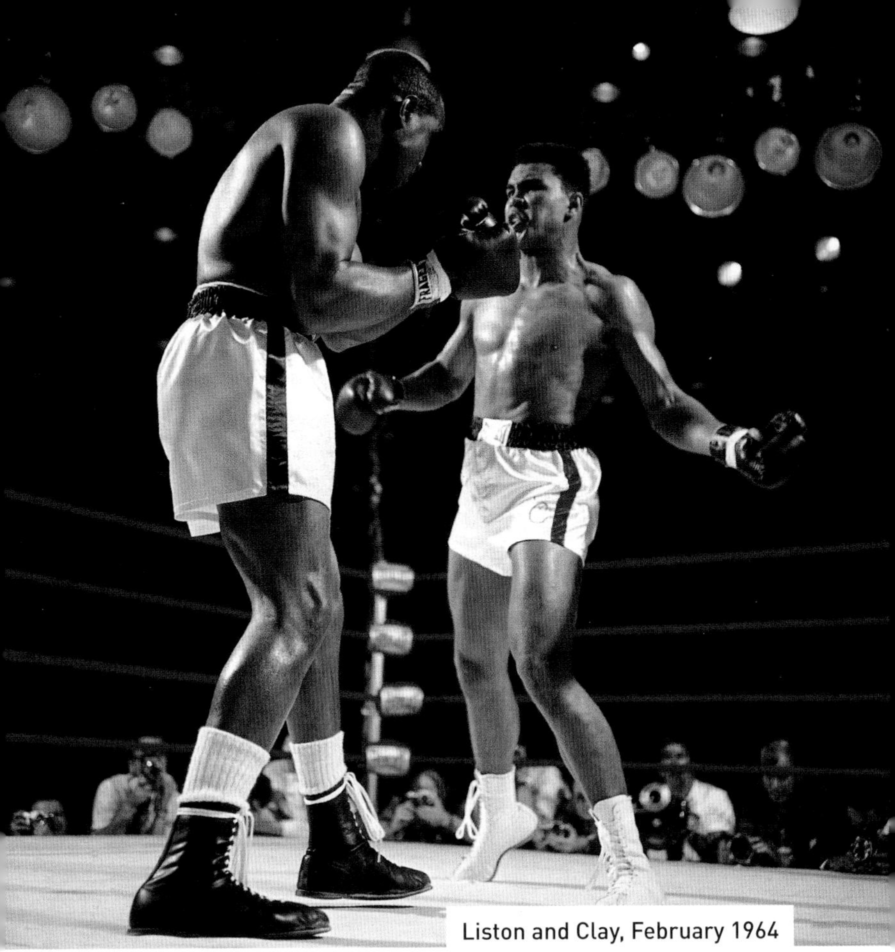

Liston and Clay, February 1964

on the gloves to stop Clay winning, he thought. Clay's trainer washed his face with water and pushed him back out into the ring. Clay could not see Liston easily at first, but he went on moving, and by Round 6, he could see much better. Now *he* was angry with Liston, and hit him with lots of good punches.

Before the start of Round 7, Liston did not want to fight any more. Cassius Clay was the winner and new World Champion – and he was only twenty-two years old! Liston did not "fall in eight." He fell in Round 7, so the words on the side of Clay's bus were wrong about that. But it did not matter to Clay. He still won!

Clay went crazy. He jumped up and down, and shouted to the reporters around the ring: "I am The Greatest!" They were surprised: Clay was the winner and not Liston. Perhaps Clay was right after all? Perhaps he was "The Greatest."

When Clay won against Liston, some people thought that it was luck. But a year later, the two men fought again, and this time, Clay knocked out Liston in Round 1. Some people in the crowd did not see any of the fight because they arrived late and were still looking for their seats when it ended!

After Clay's second fight with Liston, he won against eight more boxers. Each one of them wanted to become the World Champion, but Clay was too strong.

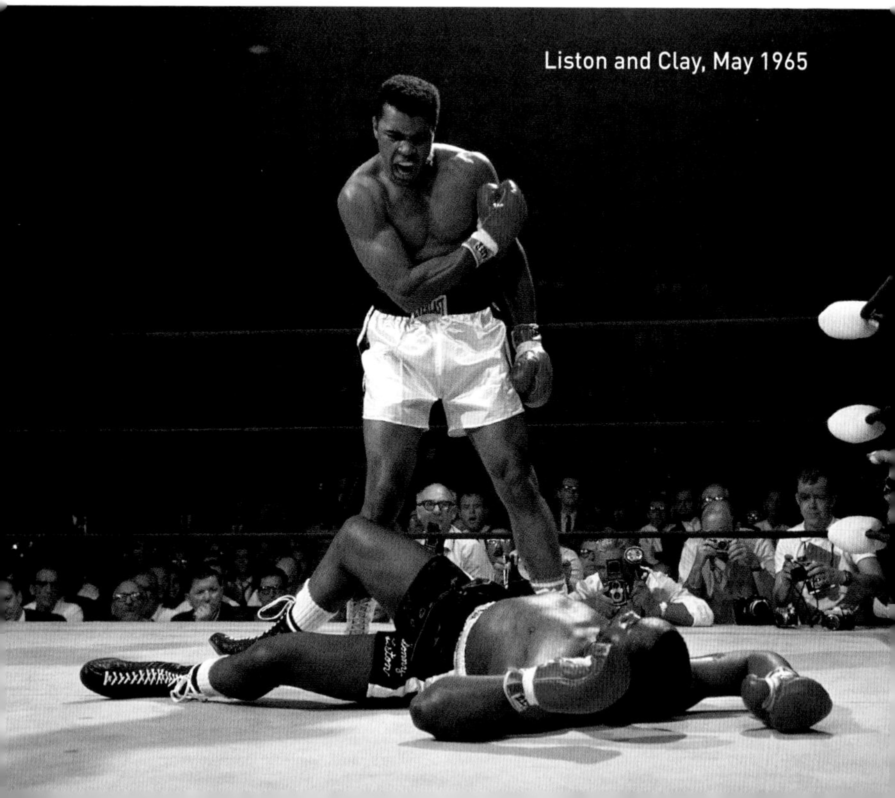

Liston and Clay, May 1965

5 Outside the ring

The 1960s were a time when many things were changing in the USA. Different groups of Americans were asking questions about their country.

Young people did not want to be like their parents. They listened to pop music by new groups like The Beatles, and wore colorful clothes. Many men had long hair. Women wanted equal rights with men, and black people wanted equal rights with white people. After Clay became the World Champion, he had a chance to speak for black people. But first, he had a surprise for everyone.

Equal rights march, Washington, 1963

Two days after his first fight with Liston, Clay talked to reporters from the newspapers and TV. He was now a Muslim, he told them. He also changed his name from Cassius Clay to Cassius X. Like his friend Malcolm X, he did this to say that he was different from white people. He explained that "Clay" was a slave name because years before, his family came to the USA from Africa as slaves, and the people who bought them gave them the name "Clay."

Two weeks after Cassius Clay became Cassius X, he changed his name again – to Muhammad Ali. This is a Muslim name. At that time in the USA, black Muslims were also talking a lot about black people's rights.

Most reporters and some other boxers did not want to call Ali by his new name. They used his old name, Cassius Clay. One boxer who used Ali's old name was Ernie Terrell. Ali was very angry with him about this. During a fight with Terrell in February 1967, Ali shouted, "What's my name?"[7] at him again and again. Some people said that Ali did not knock out Terrell because he wanted the fight to go on for longer, and he wanted to hurt him more.

It was a difficult time for Ali, and it was also a bad time for the USA. By 1965, the country was at war in Vietnam. Every year, more and more American men went there to fight. In 1966, the US army sent a letter to Ali which told him to go and fight in Vietnam. This was called a "draft" letter. Ali said that Vietnam was the white people's war and he did not want to fight against the Vietnamese people. He also said that peace was important to him, not war.

The next day, Ali's words were on the front pages of all the newspapers. It surprised a lot of people in the USA, and many of them said that Ali was not a good American. "Why does the World Champion not want to fight in Vietnam with all our other young men?" they asked.

Even a few of Ali's friends, and people from his family, wanted him to go to Vietnam. "He can just go and box for the soldiers," they said. "They'll like that. He doesn't have to hurt or kill anyone himself."

In the USA at that time, you had to go to an army center when you got a draft letter. There, you stood in line with other young men, and when you heard your name, you took a step forward. This was a way of saying, "Yes, I will fight for my country." When Ali went to the

Muhammad Ali talks to reporters inside Louisville army center, 1966

army center in Houston, Texas, all the reporters were asking the same question: "Is Ali going to take the step forward?" Ali was wearing nice clothes when he arrived at the center, so reporters thought that he was ready to go into the army.

The army officer called many men's names, and they all took a step forward. Then he shouted out Ali's old name: "Cassius Clay – Army!" It went very quiet. Ali did not move. He did not take a step forward. The officer shouted again, but Ali still did not move. He was saying to everyone that he did not want to fight in the army.

Because Ali did not want to go to Vietnam, a lot of important people in boxing across the USA said that he could not fight in their cities or call himself the World Champion any more.

Ali also had to go to court, and when he arrived at the courthouse, many people and reporters came to watch. The court took away Ali's passport. They wanted to send him to prison for five years, and they wanted him to pay ten thousand dollars, too. But Ali said to the court that he was a Muslim, and war was wrong. He said that Vietnam was not his war.

The court took three and a half

years to decide about sending Ali to prison. During that time, he could not fight. Ali had a new wife, Belinda, and a daughter, and he was worried about them. If he did not box, he could not get money for his family. He had to borrow money from friends, and he worked in a theater and on a few movies. He tried to open a burger restaurant, too, but it was not popular.

Ali goes to court, Houston, 1967

It was a difficult time for Ali, but not everyone thought that he was doing the wrong thing. By the late 1960s, many young people thought that Ali was a hero. For them, he was still the World Champion.

At this time, Martin Luther King, a very famous speaker about black rights in the USA, said that Muhammad Ali did the right thing when he said that he would not go to Vietnam. Many famous writers and thinkers in other countries agreed, and they wrote letters to Ali to say that he was right. He visited schools to speak to young people about boxing, his life as a Muslim, and the rights of black people. He was often funny. He said that talking was a lot easier than fighting, but these were not easy years for him.

Ali was very brave when he fought in the ring, but he was much braver when he said that he would not fight in Vietnam. Because of this, he lost many friends – and millions of dollars. Was this now the end of his life as a boxer?

Martin Luther King

6 "Fight of the Century"

By 1970, many other people in the USA were feeling differently about the war in Vietnam. Millions of Vietnamese people died in the war, and thousands of American soldiers, too.

In October 1970, after three and a half years, the most important court in the USA said that Muhammad Ali did not have to fight in Vietnam – or go to prison. After all that time outside the ring, he could box again. But everyone was asking, "Can Ali be as good as before? Is he still fast and strong?" Perhaps Ali was asking himself the same questions.

Ali trained hard and won his first two fights. By 1971, he was ready to fight the boxer who was now the World Champion, Joe Frazier. Ali wanted to become the World Champion again.

Frazier was shorter than Ali, but he was very strong. He was one of twelve children, and his early life was tough. From the time when he was young, he trained very, very hard. Like Ali, he had a gold medal from the Olympics – the 1964 Tokyo Games.

Before the fight, Ali and Frazier were friends. Frazier was good to Ali during the years when he could not fight. Frazier said that the court must not stop Ali boxing because it was his job. He also helped Ali with money when he was poor and, one time, drove him 150

Joe Frazier

kilometers from Philadelphia to New York City in his car. On the trip, they talked and laughed together. Frazier said that he wanted to give his baby boy Ali's old family name of "Clay."

But Ali and Frazier thought that it was good for the fight if people saw them as enemies. One time, Ali said that he wanted to go to Frazier's gym and fight him there because he could not wait for the day of the real fight. He called lots of reporters from the newspapers, radio, and TV, and told them this. They all followed his car to Frazier's gym, and soon the traffic could not move because so many people wanted to see what was happening. Ali had to walk the rest of the way to Frazier's gym. Frazier came outside, angry and ready, but the police stopped the two men from fighting in the street.

Because of all this, people were very excited about the real fight, and soon everyone wanted tickets. Each boxer got two and a half million dollars – the most money ever for a fight at that time! People called it the "Fight of the Century," and everyone was asking: "Who is going to win?" Ali was the old World Champion and Frazier was the new one. Both men always won their fights, but this time, someone had to lose.

On March 8, 1971, there were twenty thousand people in the crowd for the fight in New York City. People in fifty different countries around the world were ready to watch it on TV. Famous people – movie stars, singers, and writers – paid lots of money for seats near the boxing ring.

It was a great fight. Ali started well, but Frazier was a dangerous boxer and hit him with big punches. Each time, Ali shook his head. He wanted the crowd to know that he was not hurt.

Ali also hit Frazier, but he could not stop him, and in Round 11, Frazier hit Ali hard against the ropes. Later, in Round 15, Frazier knocked Ali down. In boxing, if the boxer lies on the floor of the ring and the referee counts to ten, it is called a "knockout" and the fight finishes. The crowd shouted loudly, and Ali got up again quickly. It was not a knockout, but it won Frazier the fight. Ali's friends were sad and surprised. In all his years as a full-time boxer, Ali never lost a fight. This was the first time ever.

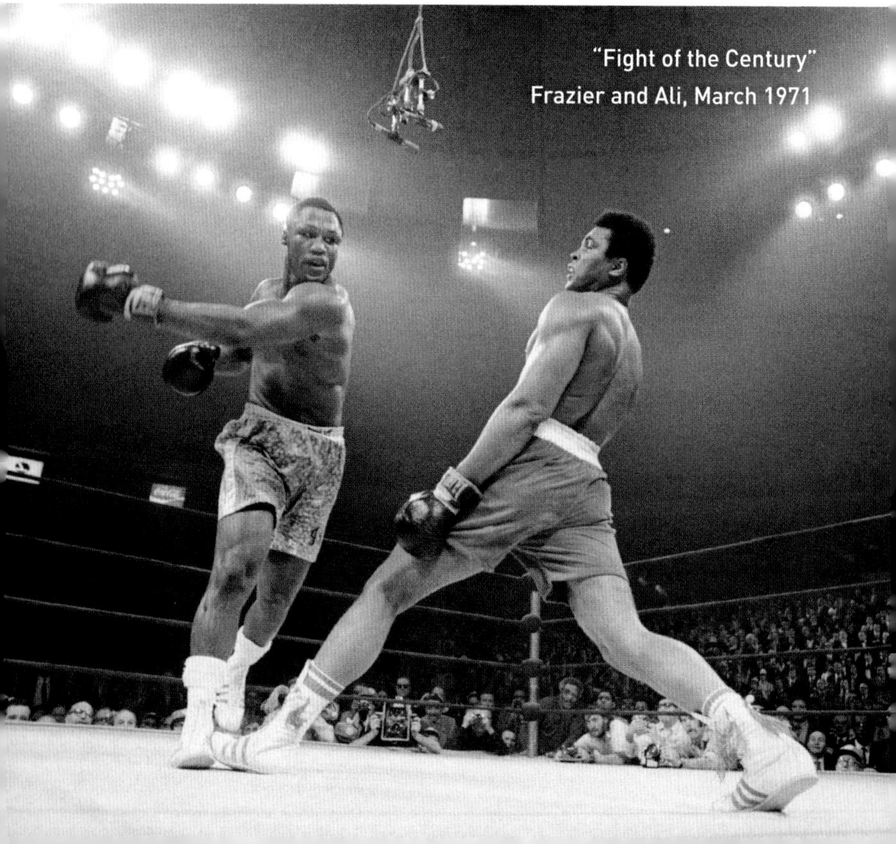

"Fight of the Century"
Frazier and Ali, March 1971

Ali and Frazier after the fight

After the fight, everyone wanted to hear what Ali thought, and the next morning, a crowd of reporters was waiting outside Ali's house. When Ali won a fight, it was easy for him to talk to them. But it was more difficult when he was the loser. His trainer went to the door to tell the reporters to go away, but Ali also went to the door. He wanted to talk to them.

"The world goes on,"[8] he told the reporters. There were many things in life that were more important, he said – and he thought that he would be a better man because he lost the fight that day.

Perhaps Ali lost against Frazier because of the years during the Vietnam War when he could not box. Was he slower after that time, and was it more difficult for him to "dance"? Or was Frazier just younger and better? Three years later, in 1974, Ali fought Frazier again. This time, Ali won. Now, each man had one win against the other... but they really were not friends any more. They were enemies inside *and* outside the ring!

7 "Rumble in the Jungle"

In the 1970s, Muhammad Ali was more famous than ever. People everywhere wanted to meet him. If he stopped in the street, there was soon a crowd around him. People wanted to touch him; they wanted his autograph. Movie stars and other famous people wanted to spend time with him. His picture was often in the newspapers, and when he was on TV, people smiled and laughed because he was funny and interesting.

By this time, Ali was also very rich. He had a big house and, like Sugar Ray Robinson, he now had a fast, expensive car – but his car was red, not pink. That was his favorite, but Ali had a lot of other cars, too. In 1972, he also built a gym for himself in the hills in Pennsylvania. All around the gym, he put big stones, and on each one was the name of a World Champion boxer in white letters: heroes from when Ali was younger, like Sugar Ray.

In 1974, the year Ali won against Joe Frazier, there was a new World Champion, a man from Texas called George Foreman. Like Ali, he also had a gold medal for boxing, from the 1968 Olympics in Mexico City.

Foreman was a mountain of a man. He was younger and bigger than Ali, he was stronger than Ali, and he had more knockouts. He trained every day with a police dog at his side, and was not afraid of anything or anyone. When Foreman fought Joe Frazier, he knocked him down six times in two rounds!

Everyone wanted to see Ali fight Foreman. "When is it going to happen, and where?" they asked. Boxing was now big business, and lots of different countries wanted the fight to happen in one of their cities. One of these countries was Zaire in Africa. Zaire is now called the Democratic Republic of Congo, and in 1974, it was a young country which wanted to show itself to the world. Zaire wanted to give five million dollars each to Foreman and Ali to bring the fight to Africa. People wanted to see a "rumble" (or fight) in the jungle of Zaire, so they called this fight the "Rumble in the Jungle"!

George Foreman with his dog

Ali was happy to go to Zaire because he wanted to make friends with black Africans. They were his people, he said. When he arrived, he stayed sixty-five kilometers outside Kinshasa, the biggest city. He opened the doors to his gym, and people could go in and watch for free – so he became more and more popular. He talked and laughed with the people, and won their hearts.

Ali in Zaire, 1974

Foreman was not a good talker like Ali, and often looked very angry. He stayed in the center of Kinshasa at a big, expensive hotel. He also took his police dog to Africa with him, so people were afraid of him.

In the days before the fight, people shouted, "Ali, *bomaye*!"[9] in the streets ("Ali, kill him!") because they wanted Ali to win. But on the day of the fight, Ali's friends and family were quiet. "What's the matter?" Ali asked them. "Do you think that I'm going to lose?" They were worried because Foreman was so strong. Ali smiled at them. "This is like another day in the gym,"[10] he said.

The fight was on October 30, 1974, and started at four o'clock in the morning. It started early because people in the USA wanted to watch it on TV during the day. Sixty thousand people were in the stadium in Kinshasa, and everyone was noisy and excited. Ali came into the ring first and waited for Foreman. Foreman took a long time to arrive, and the crowd became angry. "Ali, *bomaye*!" they shouted.

In Round 1, Ali started well. He punched Foreman with his right hand and danced around the ring. But Foreman soon punched him back, and so Ali decided to do something different. He rested against the ropes around the ring and used his arms to stop Foreman's punches. Every time Foreman came near, Ali talked to him. "They told me you could punch, George!"[11] he said.

People thought that Ali was very brave… or crazy. "Foreman is going to kill him," they said. Ali's trainer shouted "Move!" and "Dance!" but Ali stayed on the ropes. Round after round, Foreman punched Ali's body, but he did not hurt him. Slowly, Foreman got tired.

Thirty seconds before the end of Round 8, Ali changed his plan again. He came away from the ropes and then hit Foreman hard with his right hand: one, two, three, four times. Then he hit him with a fast left hand, then his right again. Foreman's head went down and his body followed. He turned around in the ring like a man who was falling into a deep, dark hole. The referee counted to ten – a knockout! Muhammad Ali was the World Champion for the second time, and the crowd went crazy! He was a hero to the people of Zaire and to people all over the world.

"Rumble in the Jungle"
Foreman and Ali, October 1974

Soon after the fight, a very strange thing happened: it began to rain hard. The weather in Zaire was usually hot and dry, but that day it rained and rained, and the boxing ring went underwater!

Foreman sat alone in his changing room. Only his trainer and his dog were with him. There was no crowd of people and he was a long way from home.

Ali did not sleep that night, or the next day. On the way back to his gym, by the side of the road through the jungle, people were shouting his name and calling to him. The men and women and children of Zaire were Ali's new friends.

When Ali got back to the USA, the American President Gerald Ford wanted to meet him. Nine years earlier, people were saying, "Ali is not a good American because he will not fight in Vietnam." Now this black man from Louisville was on his way to the White House in Washington, D.C. – the home of the US President.

Ali with President Gerald Ford

8 "Thrilla in Manila"

In 1975, a year after his fight with Foreman, Ali had the toughest fight of his life. He fought Joe Frazier for the third time. Even before the fight, there was trouble between the two men. When Ali talked, he was faster and funnier than Frazier. One day, when they were on TV together, Ali called Frazier "stupid." Frazier stood up and wanted to hit Ali, so everyone tried to stop him, and a big fight happened in front of the TV cameras.

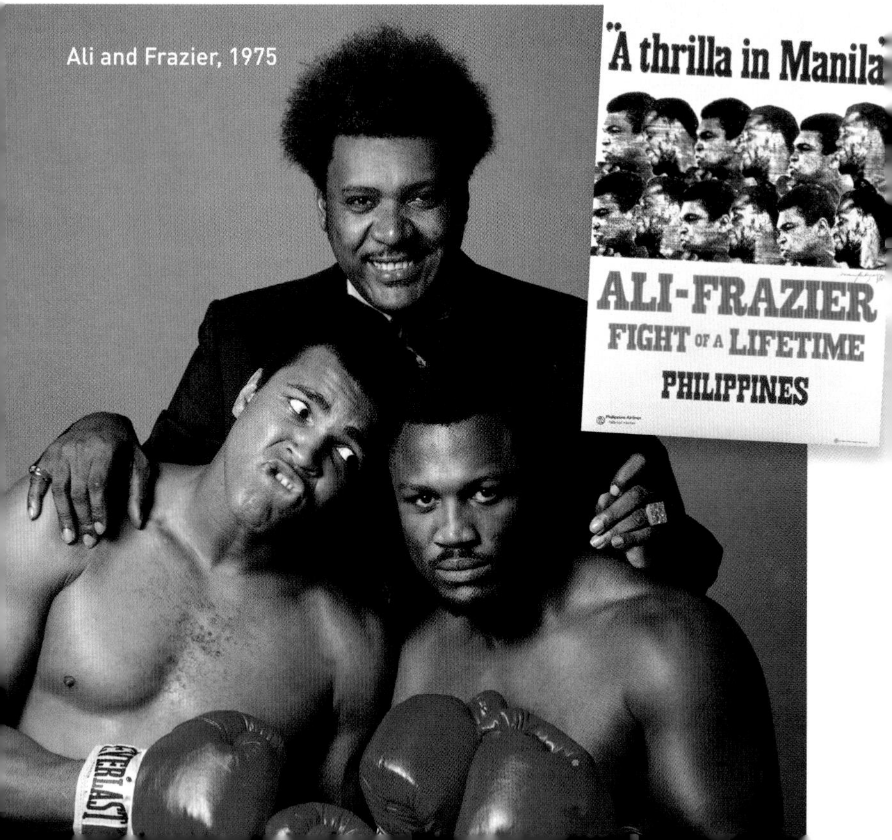

Ali and Frazier, 1975

Ali also said that Frazier was not a good black man. Frazier just wanted to please white people, Ali said. Frazier was very angry when he heard this. "I'm blacker than he is!"[12] he replied. Frazier said that he knew more about life as a poor black man in the USA than Ali. Frazier also asked why Ali had a white trainer. *His* trainer was black, not white, he said. But Ali just laughed because he knew that he was so popular.

Everyone was very excited about the fight between Ali and Frazier, and important people in many different countries wanted it to happen in one of their cities. In the end, the fight happened in the city of Manila, in the Philippines. Ali said that the fight would be a "Thrilla in Manila." The word "thriller" means something very exciting, and "Thrilla in Manila" sounds good!

As the World Champion, Ali got six million dollars to fight Frazier. A ticket for the fight itself was very expensive – more money than a year's pay for most working people in Manila. It was difficult for Ali to train well for this fight. Life was not easy for him at that time, because he and his second wife were unhappy together. But it was different for Frazier. He trained hard, away from the busy city of Manila, and he rested.

On the day of the fight, October 1, 1975, it was very hot in Manila. In the boxing ring, it was 49°C! There were thirty thousand people in the stadium, and one billion people were watching the fight on TV. The fighters' gloves were soon heavy and hard to hold up because it was so hot. Both men were older and slower now, but they were also very brave – and neither man was ready to lose. It was a great fight. Some people think that it was the best fight ever in the sport of boxing.

For thirteen rounds, each man punched the other again and again. It was very hot and they got very tired. Frazier's plan was to hit Ali's body as much as he could. "If you kill the body, the head will die," his trainer thought.

But Ali was strong, and he wanted to win. Sometimes he rested on the ropes; sometimes he threw lots of punches. Most of the time, he punched Frazier's face and, slowly, it became difficult for Frazier to see because his left eye was hurt and closing. There was also blood in his mouth.

After Round 14, just before the last round, Frazier's trainer stopped the fight. He said to Frazier, "No one will forget what you did here today."[13] When Ali saw this, he fell to the floor because he was so tired. A few minutes later, he sat up and said, "I want everyone to know that I'm the greatest fighter of all time!"[14]

After the fight, Ali and Frazier both talked to reporters. The two men looked terrible. They had black eyes and their faces were red and bloody. They could not walk easily. Ali said that he was tired and wanted to sleep for a week.

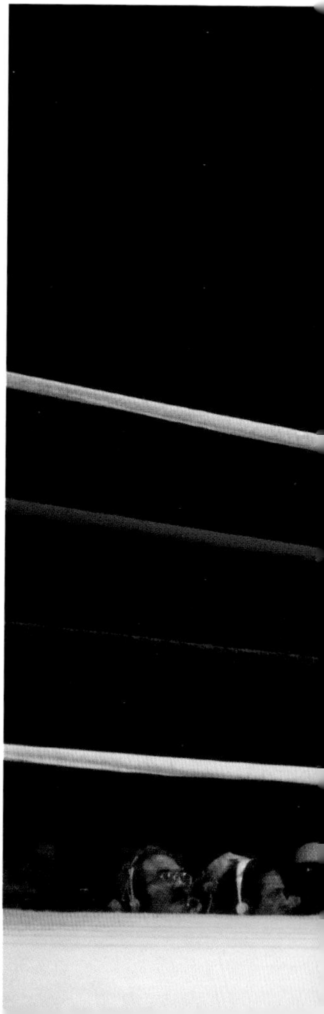

Frazier said that by the end of the fight, he could not see a thing. He looked like an empty man. The president of the Philippines described the fight as "wonderful,"[15] but Ali said that it was "the next thing to death."[16]

Much later, Ali also said that he was sorry. He wanted people to be excited about the fight, but he went too far, and he said a lot of bad things about Frazier. He hurt Frazier, and he knew that, he said. Frazier did not want to be friends with Ali again for many, many years.

"Thrilla in Manila"
Ali and Frazier, October 1975

9 Life after boxing

As the World Champion, Ali fought and won six more times before he lost to a young boxer called Leon Spinks in February 1978. "I didn't train right,"[17] Ali said after the fight.

When Ali and Spinks fought again in September that year, Ali won, and became the World Champion for the third time! He was the first person to be the World Champion three times, and it was wonderful for a boxer who was now thirty-six years old. He fought twice more, but his fight against Spinks was the last time he won in the ring.

In 1981, Ali stopped boxing. It was hard for him to say goodbye, but he was ready for something new: he wanted to work for peace and to help people around the world. "Now my life is really starting!"[18] he said happily.

In the next few years, he traveled to more than one hundred countries. He talked about peace and people's rights, and everywhere, large crowds of people came to meet him.

At this time, people were beginning to see changes in Ali. When he talked, it was sometimes hard to understand him. He moved more slowly, too, and in 1984, doctors explained to Ali that he had Parkinson's disease. When people have this disease, their body shakes and it is not easy to walk or talk. For a man like Ali, who was once so strong and fast, this was very difficult news. His life as a boxer was why he had the disease, the doctors said. It was all those thousands of punches to his head…

Ali's body was not as strong as before, but he could still think well. He was sick, but this was a new fight for him – a fight against a disease. He wanted people to know that, and he wanted to help other people to be brave, too.

Ali in 1984

In 1990, Iraq sent soldiers into Kuwait. Was war coming between the USA and Iraq? People thought so, and because there was trouble between the countries, fifteen American businessmen had to stay in Iraq as hostages of the president. They could not go back to the USA to be with their families, and were very afraid. "Perhaps they will die," people thought.

When Ali heard about the hostages, he flew to Baghdad in Iraq to try and help them. He walked the streets and met Iraqi people who all wanted his autograph. He played with children and had time for everyone: he never said "No." Ali stayed in Baghdad for ten days – even when he got very tired because he was sick. He also met the president of Iraq and asked him about the hostages. In the end, Ali went back to the USA with all fifteen of them. "What a great man!" one of the hostages said about Ali.

Ali with the hostages, 1990

In his later life, Ali gave a lot of his time and money to people who needed help. He gave away hundreds of thousands of dollars – sometimes to people in the street! Once, in Los Angeles, a soldier who fought in Vietnam wanted to jump off a building and kill himself. The police told him not to jump, but the soldier was crying because he felt so bad. Ali went up to him, put his arms around him, and brought him down from the building. Later, Ali spent money on new clothes for the man and bought a place for him to live.

In the year 2000, a group of sportspeople looked back at the last one hundred years. They wanted to decide who was "Sportsman of the Century." Ali won the competition because he did so much inside *and* outside the boxing ring. He was very happy about this, and talked about how much he enjoyed boxing and his work for peace.

Ali did not stop being world-famous in the twenty-first century. In 2001, the movie star Will Smith played him in a movie called *Ali*. The movie was about the ten years in Ali's life from when he won against Sonny Liston in 1964 to the fight against George Foreman in 1974. It also showed how Ali became a hero because he said "No" to the army during the Vietnam War.

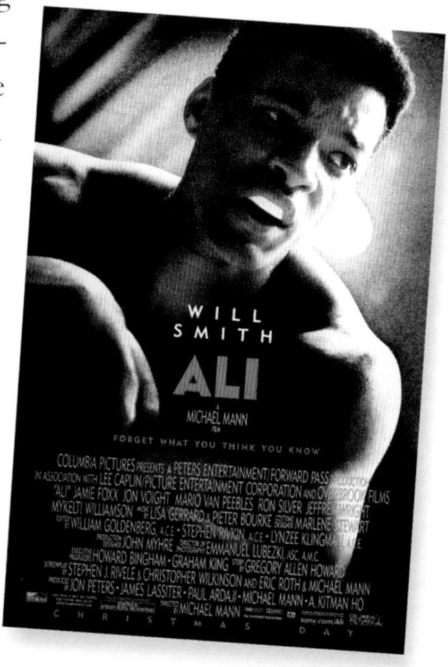

In 2005, Ali got a medal from the US president because of all his work for world peace. He got lots of medals from other people, too, but this was the most important medal in the country. In the same year, Ali opened the Muhammad Ali Center in Louisville. Here, you can find out about his life and work. The center's message is: "be great; do great things."

In 2009, Ali also opened the Muhammad Ali Parkinson Center at a hospital in Phoenix, Arizona. He wanted to use his name to help other people with this terrible disease.

Muhammad Ali Center, Louisville

In the next few years, life for Muhammad Ali was a little quieter. By this time, he had nine children. He always tried to be a good father to all of them. One of his daughters, Laila Ali, even became a World Champion boxer like her father! Ali's marriage with his fourth wife, Lonnie, was a happy one. Ali and Lonnie lived together in a place called Paradise Valley in Arizona.

Ali and his wife Lonnie

Being a good Muslim was very important for Ali. Every day, he got up early to pray and read the Koran, the Muslim holy book. Each night when he went to bed, he thought about his day. Was he proud about his life that day? he asked himself.

When Ali was at school, his reading and writing were terrible, but now he read the Koran for many hours each day, and wrote letters to the people who wrote to him. At the end of his life, he got over five thousand letters a year, and answered each one himself!

Every week, over two thousand people wanted to meet him, and he gave his autograph to every one of them. He never forgot how it felt when Sugar Ray Robinson did not give him *his* autograph that time in New York, in 1960. Ali was a tough boxer, but he was also a very kind man who loved everyone. And everyone loved him back.

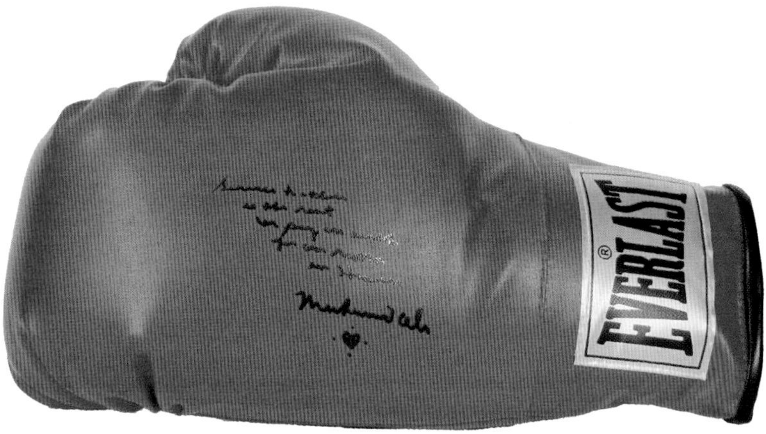

10 Remembering Ali

Ali fought against Parkinson's disease for more than thirty years, but in the end, he could not win. He died on June 3, 2016 in a hospital in Phoenix, Arizona. He was seventy-four years old.

Famous boxers Lennox Lewis and Mike Tyson and movie star Will Smith helped to put Ali's body into a big, black car. The car then drove around Ali's home city of Louisville, and thousands of people came out onto the streets to say goodbye.

They touched the car and threw flowers over it when it drove slowly down Muhammad Ali Boulevard and past Ali's first home on Grand Avenue. Buses had the words "ALI – THE GREATEST" on them.

Louisville says goodbye, June 2016

On TV, there was a lot of news about Ali, and people talked about his life both as a boxer and as a man. President Barack Obama said that Ali was bigger and brighter than anyone. "Muhammad Ali was America," he said. "Muhammad Ali will always be America. What a man."[19]

As a boxer, Ali won sixty-three of his sixty-eight fights. He was the World Champion three times, and his way of fighting was very different. Ali "danced" around the ring, but he could also hit hard and fast. Before every fight, he prayed in his corner of the ring, and when he won, he said thank you to God.

Many people today remember Muhammad Ali at the Atlanta Olympics in 1996. On that day, he held up the Olympic torch for sports, but also for people's rights and for peace and love. Later that evening in July 1996, Ali went back to his hotel in the center of Atlanta. He could not sleep, and sat in his room all night, looking out the window. He still had the torch in his hand and did not want to put it down because it was so important to him.

What was Ali thinking the next morning when he watched the sun come up slowly over Atlanta? Perhaps he was thinking about the shouts of the crowd at the stadium the day before, and his years as a great boxer. Perhaps he was remembering that young boy, Cassius Clay, who went into a gym in Louisville, came out wanting to fight… and became a hero to the world.

ERT
20 DENMAN HOUSE 20
WATERPROOFERS
AIR STREET
BANK OF SCOTLAND
CORDINGS
WEATHERPROOFS
RDINGS
THERPROOFS

GLOSSARY

autograph *(n)* when a famous person writes their name for someone

boxer *(n)* a person who does the sport of boxing (fighting against someone with your hands)

brave *(adj)* not afraid to do dangerous or difficult things

century *(n)* one hundred years

champion *(n)* a person who is the best at a sport or a game

chance *(n)* a time when something is possible / you can do something

competition *(n)* when people try to win a game, etc.

court *(n)* In a court, people decide if someone has done a crime, and what will happen to them.

crazy *(adj)* not sensible / very happy and excited

disease *(n)* When someone has a disease, they become sick.

equal *(adj)* being the same

forward *(prep)* moving to a place that is in front of you

glove *(n)* a thing that you wear on your hand

God *(n)* Religious people believe in a god, or gods, that they cannot see.

gym *(n)* a room or building for doing sports

hero *(n)* a person who has done something brave or good

holy *(adj)* very special because it is about a god or gods

hostage *(n)* a person that someone keeps as a prisoner because they want something

jungle *(n)* a forest in a hot part of the world

knock out *(v)* in boxing, when you knock a person to the floor and they can't get up; **knockout** *(n)*

medal *(n)* A medal is round and made of metal; you get it when you do something very good, e.g. win a competition.

message *(n)* words from one person to another

Muslim *(n)* a person who follows the religion of Islam

officer *(n)* a person in the army or police who tells other people what to do

peace *(n)* when there is no fighting between people or countries

popular *(adj)* liked by a lot of people

pray *(v)* to speak to a god or gods

president *(n)* the leader of a country that has no king or queen

pretty *(adj)* nice to look at

proud *(adj)* when you have something or do something and are pleased with it

punch *(v & n)* to hit somebody or something hard with your closed hand (your fist)

referee *(n)* a person who watches a game or a sport and stops the players doing anything wrong

reporter *(n)* a person who writes in a newspaper or speaks on the radio or television about things that have happened

rights *(n)* what people can have and do, e.g. the right to speak freely

ring *(n)* the place where boxers fight

ropes *(n)* the strong lines that go around a boxing ring to stop the boxers falling out of it

round *(n)* one part of a game or competition

slave *(n)* a person who belongs to another person and must work for that person for no money

stadium *(n)* a very big place with seats around it for watching sports

step *(n)* when you move your foot up and put it forward or backward

tough *(adj)* very strong or difficult

train *(v)* to teach a person or an animal to do something / to do something a lot because you want to be good at it

war *(n)* fighting between countries or between groups of people

The life of Muhammad Ali

1942

Born Cassius Clay in Louisville, USA, on January 17.

1954

Begins boxing at 12 years old.

1960

Wins a gold medal at Rome Olympics.

1975

Wins against Joe Frazier in the "Thrilla in Manila."

1978

Wins against Leon Spinks and becomes World Champion for the third time.

1981

Stops boxing to travel the world and do peace work / help people.

1984

Hears from doctors that he has Parkinson's disease.

1996

Lights the Olympic flame in Atlanta.

2000

Becomes "Sportsman of the Century."

flame *(n)* the smallest part of a fire

1964

Wins against Sonny Liston and becomes World Champion for the first time. Becomes a Muslim and changes his name to Muhammad Ali.

1966

Gets a draft letter from the US army for the Vietnam War.

1967

Has to stop boxing because he does not want to fight in the Vietnam War.

1970

Starts boxing again.

1971

Loses to Joe Frazier in the "Fight of the Century."

1974

(January) Wins against Joe Frazier. (October) Wins against George Foreman in the "Rumble in the Jungle" and becomes World Champion for the second time.

2001

Ali the movie plays at theaters.

2005

Gets the Presidential Medal of Freedom. Opens the Muhammad Ali Center in Louisville, USA.

2009

Opens the Muhammad Ali Parkinson Center in Phoenix, USA.

2016

Dies in Phoenix, USA, on June 3.

Think ahead

1 **Read the back cover. What are you going to read about in this book?**

- boxing ☐
- being famous ☐
- peace ☐
- cars ☐
- technology ☐
- black people ☐
- the Olympics ☐

2 **What do you know about Muhammad Ali? Choose the correct words to complete the sentences.**

1 Muhammad Ali was a famous *movie star / boxer.*
2 He was born and lived in the *USA / UK.*
3 He was the World Champion *two / three* times.
4 He *had / did not have* an exciting life.
5 He died in the *twentieth / twenty-first* century.

3 **RESEARCH** **Find out the answers to these questions about boxing.**

1 When was boxing first in the Olympic Games as a sport?
2 What are the "Marquess of Queensberry Rules"?

Chapter check

CHAPTER 1 **Complete the sentences with the correct words.**

hero peace rights stadium torch

1 The sports __________ for the 1996 Olympics was in Atlanta, Georgia.
2 Muhammad Ali brought the Olympic __________ into the stadium at the 1996 Olympics.
3 Black people's __________ were very important to Ali.
4 All his life, Ali fought for __________ and against war.
5 Ali was a __________ to a lot of people because of what he did inside and outside the boxing ring.

CHAPTER 2 **Are these sentences true or false?**

1 When Cassius's brother, Rudolph, threw stones at him, he usually hit him.
2 Because he was black, Cassius could not get a drink of water from a restaurant.
3 Cassius went into a gym to look for a bicycle thief.
4 Cassius's first fight was against a boy from Louisville.
5 Corky Baker was a very strong boxer from Chicago.
6 Before he was eighteen, Cassius won a lot of fights and competitions.

CHAPTER 3 **Put the sentences in the correct order, 1–6.**

a Cassius met the boxer Sugar Ray Robinson in New York.

b Cassius said hello to everybody when he arrived in the Olympic village.

c A large crowd met Cassius in Louisville.

d Cassius walked round Times Square with his medal.

e Cassius won the Olympic gold medal against a Polish boxer called Pietrzykowski.

f Cassius saw a black man in the street with a piece of paper which said "BUY BLACK."

CHAPTER 4 **Correct the underlined words.**

1 Cassius Clay loved fighting with words.

2 During his fight with Archie Moore, Clay said that he would win in Round 4.

3 Early one morning, Clay drove a bus to Liston's gym.

4 Malcolm X was like a father to Clay.

5 Clay said that there was something on Liston's hands which burned his eyes.

6 Clay became the World Champion when he was twenty-seven years old.

CHAPTER 5 Choose the correct answers.

1 Two days after the fight with Liston, Cassius Clay changed his name to … .
a Cassius X b Malcolm X c Muhammad Ali

2 In 1966, the US army sent Ali a … .
a passport b draft letter c medal

3 Ali did not want to go and fight in Vietnam, because he said that … was important to him.
a boxing b family c peace

4 At the army center, Ali did not … .
a step forward b step back c stand still

5 The court wanted to send Ali to … for five years.
a Vietnam b Texas c prison

CHAPTER 6 Match the sentence halves.

1 In October 1970, …
2 In 1971, …
3 In Round 15 of the fight, …
4 In 1974, …

a the court said that Ali did not have to go to prison.
b Ali fought Frazier again, and this time, he won.
c Ali fought the new World Champion, Joe Frazier.
d Frazier knocked Ali down, and Ali lost the fight.

CHAPTER 7 **Choose the correct words to complete the sentences.**

1 In the 1970s, Muhammad Ali was often *on TV* / *in movies.*

2 George Foreman trained every day with *another famous boxer* / *a police dog.*

3 The "Rumble in the Jungle" happened in *Zaire* / *the USA.*

4 Most of the people in the crowd wanted *Ali* / *Foreman* to win.

5 In Round 8, *Foreman* / *Ali* won with a knockout.

6 Ali met the US President in *Louisville* / *Washington, D.C.*

CHAPTER 8 **Check (✓) the three sentences which are true.**

1 In 1975, Muhammad Ali had his first fight against Joe Frazier. ☐

2 The fight happened in the city of Manila, in the Philippines. ☐

3 The fight was called the "Thrilla in Manila." ☐

4 On the day of the fight, it was 45°C in the boxing ring. ☐

5 Frazier's trainer stopped the fight before Round 15 because Frazier was so badly hurt. ☐

6 After the fight, Ali and Frazier were friends for many years. ☐

CHAPTER 9 **Answer the questions.**

1 Who did Muhammad Ali win against before he stopped boxing?
2 How many times was Muhammad Ali the World Champion?
3 Where did Ali go in 1990 to help American hostages?
4 What important competition did Ali win in 2000?
5 Who was in the 2001 film about Ali?
6 Why did Ali get a medal in 2005?
7 What did he open in 2005?
8 How many letters did Ali get every year at the end of his life?

CHAPTER 10 **Complete the sentences with the correct names.**

Barack Obama *Lennox Lewis* *Mike Tyson*
Muhammad Ali *Will Smith*

1 ____________ died on June 3, 2016, in Phoenix, Arizona.
2 ____________, ____________, and ____________ helped to put Ali's body in a big, black car.
3 ____________ said that Ali was bigger and brighter than anyone.

Focus on vocabulary

1 Look at the picture and write the words for 1–6.

boxer corner crowd glove ring ropes

2 Complete the report with the words below.

Champion dance hero punches Round

In ________ 8, Ali came off the ropes and started to ________. Foreman could not stop Ali's ________. He went down, and the referee counted to ten: a knockout. Ali was the winner and the World ________ for the second time. The people of Zaire had a new ________.

Focus on language

1 Complete the sentences with *to* or *that*. You only need to complete one gap in each sentence.

1 Cassius asked __________ his brother Rudolph __________ throw stones at him.
2 The US army told __________ Ali __________ fight in the Vietnam War.
3 Ali said __________ talking __________ was a lot easier than fighting.
4 Doctors explained __________ to Ali __________ he had Parkinson's disease.

2 DECODE Read the text from the story and underline *his* and *them*. Then answer the questions.

Two days after his first fight with Liston, Clay talked to reporters from the newspapers and TV. He was now a Muslim, he told [1]them. He also changed his name from Cassius Clay to Cassius X. Like his friend Malcolm X, he did this to say that he was different from white people. He explained that "Clay" was a slave name because years before, his family came to the USA from Africa as slaves, and the people who bought [2]them gave [3]them the name "Clay."

1 Who does each use of *his* refer to?
2 Who does *them* refer to in…
 a use 1? b uses 2 and 3?

Discussion

1 Read the dialogue. Do you agree with speaker A or speaker B?

A: I think that Ali was a great boxer because he was angry about the world. He took that anger to the boxing ring and he used it.

B: Really? I'm not sure. The way I see it, he was a great boxer because he wanted to be "The Greatest," not because he was angry.

A: But what about his fight with Ernie Terrell? He was angry then.

B: OK, that's true. He was angry then. But mostly, I think that he just wanted to be the best.

2 Complete the phrases from exercise 1.

1 I ___________ that…
2 Really? I'm ___________.
3 The ___________ I ___________ it, …
4 But what ___________…?
5 OK, that's ___________.

3 Which of the phrases 1–5 in exercise 2 are used to…

a give your opinion?

b disagree?

c agree?

d question the other person?

4 THINK CRITICALLY Which of these statements do you agree with the most? Why?

I think that Ali was "The Greatest" because of…

a his boxing wins.

b his fight for black people's rights.

c his work for people with Parkinson's disease.

d his fight for peace.

e the kind things that he did.

5 COMMUNICATE Find someone who gave a different answer to exercise 4. Discuss the question below with them. Use the phrases in exercise 2.

Why was Ali "the Greatest"?

1 Read about the tennis player Serena Williams. Answer the questions below.

Early years

Serena Williams was born in Saginaw, Michigan, USA, on September 26, 1981. She started playing tennis when she was only three years old, in Los Angeles. When she was nine, the family moved to Florida, and Serena and her sister, Venus, went to a special tennis school. Serena's father, Richard, was her trainer and taught her at home from 1995. He wanted Serena to be good at tennis *and* her school subjects! He thought that some people in the world of tennis were not kind to his daughters because they were black.

First big win and "Serena Slam"

Serena won her first big "Grand Slam" tournament (competition) in 1999. This was the US Open. In 2002, she became world number one. In 2003 (and again in 2015), she was champion of all four "Grand Slam" tournaments at the same time. People called this a "Serena Slam"!

Great champion

Serena went on to win many important tournaments playing on her own (singles) and with her sister Venus (doubles). She also won four Olympic gold medals. People say that she changed the sport of women's tennis because she hit the ball so hard and fast.

1 Where was this champion born?
2 When did he/she start to play his/her sport?
3 When did he/she win his/her first important competition?
4 Why did he/she become so famous?

2 **Think of another champion from any sport. Answer the questions above about this person.**

3 **CREATE Use the answers from exercise 2 to write a short text about your champion.**

4 **COLLABORATE In small groups, talk about the champions you have chosen. Then, as a group, decide which champion is "The Greatest," and why.**

REFERENCES

1 *The Soul of a Butterfly* by Muhammad Ali (2004), p.13
2 *The Soul of a Butterfly* (Ali, 2004), p.13
3 *The Soul of a Butterfly* (Ali, 2004), pp.31–32
4 *The Greatest – My Own Story* by Muhammad Ali (1975), pp.65–69
5 *Sport: Louisville Lip* (1962, Nov 23) *Time* magazine. Retrieved March 14, 2017, from http://content.time.com/time/magazine/article/0,9171,829490,00.html
6 *The Greatest – My Own Story* (Ali, 1975), p.100
7 *Ernie Terrell: Boxer who won a world title but suffered a savage beating after inadvertently calling Muhammad Ali Cassius Clay* by Steve Bunce (2014, Dec 28) *The Independent*. Retrieved March 14, 2017 from http://www.independent.co.uk/news/people/ernie-terrell-boxer-who-won-a-world-title-but-suffered-a-savage-beating-after-inadvertently-calling-9947176.html
8 *Muhammad Ali – His Life and Times* by Thomas Hauser (1991), p.233
9 *Ali boma ye: The chant that made Muhammad Ali an African hero* (2016, June 7) *The Week*. Retrieved March 14, 2017 from http://www.theweek.co.uk/muhammad-ali/73369/ali-boma-ye-the-chant-that-made-muhammad-ali-an-african-hero
10 *Muhammad Ali – His Life and Times* (Hauser, 1991), p.273
11 *Ali – The Greatest of All Time* (6 Disc Collector's Edition, ESPN). As related by Archie Moore (in Foreman's corner)
12 *Muhammad Ali – His Life and Times* (Hauser, 1991), p.314
13 *Joe Frazier: Still Smokin' after all these years* (2008, Nov) Retrieved March 14, 2017 from http://www.telegraph.co.uk/culture/3563084/Joe-Frazier-Still-Smokin-after-all-these-years.html
14 *Thrilla in Manila post fight* (2013, Apr). Retrieved March 14, 2017 from https://www.youtube.com/watch?v=MA8D2PMi7G4
15 *Thrilla in Manila post fight* (2013, Apr). Retrieved March 14, 2017 from https://www.youtube.com/watch?v=MA8D2PMi7G4

16 *The Greatest – My Own Story* (Ali, 1975), p.415
17 *Muhammad Ali – His Life and Times* (Hauser, 1991), p.353
18 *Muhammad Ali – His Life and Times* (Hauser, 1991), p.514
19 *Muhammad Ali funeral: Rousing farewell at Louisville memorial* (2016, June 10) BBC News. Retrieved March 14, 2017 from http://www.bbc.co.uk/news/world-us-canada-36496473

If you liked this Bookworm, why not try...

The Olympic Games

STAGE 2
Alex Raynham

Every four years, the world's best athletes come together for one of the most exciting competitions in sport: the Olympic Games. After years of training, competitors in more than forty different sports win and lose their events, and set new world records, in front of crowds of people. The Olympic Games are more than two thousand five hundred years old. So how did they start, how have they changed over the years, and what have been some of the most important times in their history?

Martin Luther King

STAGE 3
Alan C. McLean

The United States in the 1950s and 60s was a troubled place. Black people were angry, because they did not have the same rights as whites. It was a time of angry words, of marches, of protests, a time of bombs and killings. But above the angry noise came the voice of one man – a man of peace. 'I have a dream,' said Martin Luther King, and it was a dream of blacks and whites living together in peace and freedom. This is the story of an extraordinary man, who changed American history in his short life.
